Essavadore

The Skifakore Truth Project
The Film Synopsis

Act 1

We find ourselves with Kerry onboard a ferry from Ireland to the welsh port of Fishguard. Kerry, twenty years of age, muscular build, sharp brown eyes to match his long brown hair. He looked rather weathered in his dark black coat, along with his standard army issue steel toe cap boots. Usually, quite a cheery chap but with troubles aplenty. It's late in the month of October, getting colder every day and the ferry crossing is a rough one. Kerry walks the decks thinking to himself, *"why did it come to this?"*

You see, the story started the previous Christmas. It started in the usual way with all the family coming around for presents and cheer. It had been snowing in the evening and turned into a white Christmas day. His brother and two sisters where playing in the snow out back and he went to join them, building snowmen and snow forts for snowball fights and as always, the girls won every round. Unknown to everyone it would be the last Christmas they would all spend together,

It went the usual way, presents in the morning then just waiting for dinner with all the trimmings. You cannot beat home cooking, they all say. Time for photographs around the fireplace with a roaring log fire for the night. They placed the camera on a tripod so they could all get in with a ten second delay, that was just about achieved with a few laughs. A happy time for everyone. That night Kerry's father suffered a massive heart attack and passed away. He was always the backbone of the family. A proud man who had given forty years to the building trade. He started out cleaning and sweeping floors and by the time he retired was head foreman for a major building company. So sadly, the family drifted apart.

From that point, Kerry's mother started suffering depression and fell into cycles of mental illness. He did his best to support her through the rough times putting his own life on hold to see his two sisters and brother grow up. In a way, taking the place of his father, as he was the eldest of the children.

It's very much a cold dark and rainy night, Kerry is slumped on the deck chair, soaking wet from the rain dripping off his green corduroy hat. His father becoming a fast-distant memory and at this thought Kerry's muscles tense in his face as the tears start to fall, for his father.

He stands and begins pacing five steps forward five steps back his whole body starting to seize with the cold, rain and wind. What is at the end of this ferry crossing? No one to meet, no one to see him safe, just looking for a new life away from his demons that haunt his every step as his tears are hidden in the rain.

When his father passed away, he promised he would take care of the family and as there was no work in the small village in Ireland, seeks forth to the mainland for better prospects.

So here we have Kerry, twenty-five pounds in his pocket, two days of clothes in his backpack and four cheese and onion sandwiches, As he rummages for the sandwiches, he finds a parcel from his mother and opens it he discovers his father's note book, worn brown leather bound with a green ribbon. As Kerry reads, a new light falls on his father's past. The similarities are uncanny. His father passed away when he was fourteen. John, Kerry's father, took the same ferry to the mainland but John did not find any work so enlisted in the navy, ending up on H.M.S Belfast, just before world war two broke out.

Kerry reads on in the shelter of the ferry café having queued twenty minutes for a, less then hot, coffee. He was greatly annoyed and grimaced at every mouthful. So, he reads how his father escorted merchant ships across the Atlantic, always on the lookout for U boats. A picture falls out, a photograph of the crew rescuing a sailing ship that had capsized. A memory never told as John was not particularly proud of his service in the war. Kerry reads on in the dim light of the battered ferry.

The year nineteen forty-three, a merchant ship was just hit by a torpedo and was ablaze lighting up the night sky. H.M.S Belfast pulls up alongside, to rescue the survivors John writes how he witnessed charcoaled bodies on the decks, some still on fire and screaming men running towards him in desperation. What he had seen will never leave him. There were only five men out of twenty-five rescued and it would take years for John to forget the smell of charcoaled body's. Then the hunt was on for the U Boat. Depth charges were sent over the side in the trail of the torpedo that was seen and it's not long till oil and debris is floating by as the U boat was hit.

Kerry, reading this with some disbelief finds a new admiration for his departed father. Kerry, thinking to himself *"if my father can survive like this I should not worry"* and a peace falls upon Kerry. The tears were no more.

Act 2

Something catches Kerry's eye. Glancing up from reading the journal, in the dim light, two bright hazel eyes meet him. A woman with flowing red hair.

She says, "hello there."

Kerry is transfixed on these beautiful eyes staring back at him.

She says, "my name is Louise. What's yours?"

Kerry chokes slightly. He had never seen an angel but *"I have now"* he thinks to himself.

"Kerry" He replies, "What brings you onboard this ferry?" Kerry asks.

Louise replies, "Down on my luck, looking for work on the mainland."

"Same here. We're two peas in a pod, so to say." A light smile and then his answer

"Maybe we could team up?" Kerry splutters.

Louise, now with a wide grin, "Maybe. I have been watching you as you seem engrossed in that journal. You wish to share with me. Kerry?"

"It's my father's memories and some nightmares he lived with for years without telling anyone."

The dim light begins to flicker, they both glance out of the window. A faint light through the rain clouds moving away. The sun is coming up on the new day.

Louise says "I think we could have something special me and you."

Kerry replies "we will be docking soon and a start of a new life. One day at a time, we should take this, we will be a good team. You are the most beautiful angel I have ever seen.

Louise slightly laughs, looks Kerry in the eye and says, "Love at first sight is never easy we take things steady and everything will work out."

Both huddle in the corner of the café, away from everything and let the past go. Looking forward to a new life as coincidence brings them together. We were never born to walk this life alone. This night will never fade as two lovers find each other and take chances for only the brave.

The tannoy crackles into life

"we will be docking at Fishguard in roughly thirty minutes. We hope you have had a pleasant journey and will travel with us again".

"Let's go out to the deck." Kerry leads Louise out. The wind was cold, sharp and brisk but the rain has stopped and the sun was rising as a promise of a warm day.

Kerry: "I can see land. Not long now," as he points out to the hazy horizon. "Louise take my hand." They move closer. Kerry faces Louise with a slight smile "Kiss me," he says. A full embrace like holding on to life, they kiss for the first time. A overwhelming air of contentment surrounds them as a ray of light dances over them across the open waters. As time slips away into the moment of love.

Kerry: "We're docking. Do you have any plans?"

Louise: "Yes. I was going to make my way to Cardiff. I have friends at university there. They have a shared house close to town.

A smile from Kerry.

"I'll tag along then."

Louise's eyes lit up and she kisses Kerry's cheek.

"Yes of course silly, but we both need to find work and pay our way.

So here we find ourselves, a chance meeting of fate. Maybe Karma, correcting the downs as they say you cannot appreciate what you have if you have never been without.

The ferry docking at Fishguard. in the bright sunshine of a crisp autumn day. The sky is bright, with golden glare of a new sun. The bows of the ship opened and the gang planks lowered as we see two new young lovers take their first steps into a new life of optimism. Knowing their life will be difficult but brave enough to take chances. This ferry crossing will never be forgotten.

Act 3

"Kerry I am Terraustrall. We need to talk with your species. Your dimensions are imbalanced. You have been disturbing peace in the equilibrium of your planet by pollution and exploitation and death upon thousands. This time continuum cannot continue this way. Earth is imbalanced in assets, in movement of the basic atoms that hold life together. With this, you have been opening portals to unmentionable dangers. By doing this exploration, it has awakened our feelings. You now need our help before it is too late. We have seeded life for eternity. You are our children, as we influence you in impassive guidance but now we need to be direct. The time to reveal our influence has come to this time. The fact is that your humanity will cease to exist if we leave your kind to carry this self-destruction of your God, of what you dwell on, in above and below. Kerry we need to communicate through your presence, to mankind. Reading in your dreams, we can communicate learn explore your feelings, as we guide your soul."

"Kerry! Wake up, Kerry. We're here." Louise softly stroked Kerry's forehead,

"Who are you?"

"I'm Louise, silly. "We met on the ferry. Remember? We're in Cardiff. Time to wake up.

Kerry awoke slowly, in a cold sweat.

"I have a choice." He said.

Louise: "A choice? What are you on about?"

Kerry: "I had a vision. Terraustrall came to me. I think I'm losing my mind. I need to make notes."

They alighted from the train and sat on the platform. There was an old busker playing Johnny Cash numbers. He stopped and stared at Kerry and said,

"The horsemen are coming. Open your eyes, young one."

Louise gathers Kerry up. "Let's get out of here. My friends are not far, Senghennydd Rd. We need some descent coffee."

As they walked, the darkest storm clouds came across the city turning day into night. Lightning sparked the clouds. Kerry could hear whispers, *"We will save mankind do not be afraid."*

"Did you hear that Lou?"

"No, I did not." said Louise "what was it?"

"Nothing" Kerry thought for a while. "I need a smoke." He lit up. Experience comes to everyone eventually.

Pondering life, he asked "Lou, do you believe in God?

"Sometimes." said Louise "Why are you asking that, Kerry?"

"Just a few things." he said "I think I have a greater purpose in life I need help to find the way. That is not unique"

Louise took Kerry by the hand "Follow me."

They came to rows of Victorian terraced houses. Every garden with black bin bags all the way down the street. Number 212 had a raw wooden door and ornate Victorian tiles.

Knock knock! Lou pushes the door open. "Hello? Anyone there? Hey! It's Jenny!"

Lou hugs the woman who is Dr Jennifer French head of Neuroscience and the Mental Health Research Institute at the university.

"Who's this, then? Louise's potential husband?"

"No, my new beau, Kerry. Love at first sight. I'm telling you the truth."

Kerry was a bit uneasy as he see's shadows of wings behind Jennifer.

"Hello" says Kerry.

"You look a bit pale sweetheart, let's get you in and a nice cup of tea." Jenny takes Kerry to the kitchen.

Hours pass as Lou catches up on all the news. Dr white walks in, "Hello everyone. What's been happening here in a room full of smoke and empty cups?"

"Open the window, dear." Dr Susan White says to Jen.

Susan, my dear, you're so bossy. Meet Kerry fresh off the boat from Ireland, who would be a fantastic guinea pig" Jen winks at Lou.

"What do you mean?" says Kerry

"Well your family history." says Jen. "We need people like you for our research programme of DNA study's.

"I would be more than willing." Kerry agreed.

"We will need to see you in the lab. It will take quite a few hours at a time. We can make you comfortable here with us and we will keep you fed and watered. Come with me, both of you. I will show you your room." Susan led them upstairs to the spare room "This will do. Mind you keep your door closed. Jen is a bit of a vampire." Sue winks. "Bloods tomorrow, get some sleep my dears."

Kerry wakes in a cold sweat at three am. He was not quite awake but hears a voice in the attic.

"Kerry, I'm Stag. Don't be alarmed we're the surveillance team for you."

Kerry sleepily says "What? Why?"

A different voice comes back "We have seen things you would not believe, you need to relax" Kerry falls back to sleep, thinking he is dreaming.

"Morning Pearls!" Susan walks in. "Can we interview you today, Kerry? up and at them. Bathroom is free."

He walks around in a bit of a daze for the rest of the morning. Even the coffee is making him tired.

Jennifer sits at the kitchen table with a note pad. Kerry come and sit and tell me about your family."

A few hours pass and Kerry feels like he is being interrogated.

"OK then, just some blood now." says Jen as she gets her medical kit out. "It won't hurt and we can use this to map your D.N.A and compare with over three thousand profiles. It's mostly automated."

The news is on the television. A report on Light Solar. The Atom Zero Point project by NASA are due to test their new engines that work on Polyatomic Ion Electromagnetic Pulses.

"That's a mouthful." he thinks.

Act 4

This Is the turning point for the Human Race. Unbeknown to anyone these engines will lead to the destruction of humanity.

Lou looks out of the window "The weathers bad again."

Kerry grunts and looks at her seeing wings again in the shadows. "I don't feel well, Lou. I'm not OK, really struggling. I'm seeing things that are not there and hearing voices in the attic."

Lou says "Well we're in the right place all you need is love, Kerry. I will talk to Jen."

Latitude 84° S Longitude 163° E, We Berithdawe, gather the stones of age to Mount Sirius, fledglings the guidance upon you. Our caverns come to air. To breathe life upon century's in sleep. Mankind becomes clear. We bring peace upon you.

"Where am I? Who am I? Berithdawe? What do you want from me?" As Kerry wakes from sleeping on the sofa, Jen walks in.

"Lou talked to me. What's going on with you then?" She asks.

"I have no idea. I keep hearing and seeing things. I'm scared, Jen."

Well you told me about your family history. Do you do drugs Kerry?

"I have" he says.

"Well you have expanded your mind to access a greater universe that surrounds us. We need to be careful with you as the world is about to change, Duirsail has told me of the coming worlds of Essavadore, Igconnegativy will bring us hope according to the stones of age, Earth is changing and will change quite rapidly. A cleansing of the waters of life. They have told me you are the contact for Terraustrall. Pray for guidance Kerry, God has his ways, peace be with you.

"Am I losing my mind, Jen?"

"No! Far from this, you are opening the dimensions of the Skifakore we need you with us and God has sent you. Mind sets are in chastity free yourself from your conditioning. This comes to freedom and freedom of the mind. The Dipole has been effected by NASA there Is no going back now. The Earth is changing. The axis we have known, they bought forward Rhyolite Nova the warrior races of the 24th dimensions they will bring mankind to be extinct If the door Is not closed. We have to gather the messages from our speakers. Electroconsive languages activated from the atom zero point, where the Earth orbit fails our world can reset the problems but we need believers such as you. As you can now understand Kerry."

"Stop, stop! I don't understand!" Beads of sweat formed on Kerry's face, his muscles become tensioned. "Stop! I don't want this! I'm not special! I'm not a hero!" He falls to the floor in tears.

"Lou, hold me. Hold me now. All I want is sleep."

"There is no running from this, Kerry" Lou turns to hold him. "From birth, Kerry. they have been with us. Guidance is their keys. The Earth is undergoing major changes rapidly now they wish for our species not to die out. We are all miracles in this universe. Life within life multiple sequences connected combined. The

Skifakore are the languages of God of that it is mathematics."

"Lou, I'm sorry. It makes no sense but it does at the same time." Said Kerry.

Terraustrall, "We are heroes in complete circles. In many dimensions"

"They have come to help with our transformation. For the love of our Mothers, Skifakore are not allowed to come in physical form. It takes a great deal of their energy to communicate. They have been where we are. They are not the only ones. It's infinite. The twin flames of life are dimming after twenty thousand years at the centre of our universe, on the parallel of the life force, there are great planetary movements. Not to be measured in days. We cannot comprehend this time line. We are the star children."

"Worlds of Pedrllehart hear me now I have spoken through Louise for many years, Kerry wake up for the love that is all around you. We are the way forward. Dr Jen we need to get this message out over the internet please help."

Jen: "I know Nicholas In the IT Department at the university. I will ask him. Maybe global software that would give the message to everyone logging on to the internet, and through their phones." Jen, Telephones Nicholas

"This Is not propaganda, Nicholas. This is the death of the Earth. We need populations to wake up to protect themselves from the coming events that man has unleashed on himself."

Nicholas, "An internet worm like ransomware. If we could infect enough systems with this message, it would make mainstream media but we need to keep the message simple."

"Earth is in Death. Gather Your local community to survive. Prepare for life changes, global changes". Messengers of Skifakore. It will take a few days Jen I will get right on this."

Terraustrall, "Kerry, the twin flames of Essavadore are burning out for your dimension. You hold the key and I tell you this. We are not allowed to take physical form in this dimension but Duirsail, many century's ago, fell In love with a woman in your family line and you are the last of your generations. You are the key to past dimensions. We could evacuate the Earth to our worlds that we have seeded. The fact is Kerry, you will not survive the energy gateway. This will only take moments but it will rip you apart, scattering you to the universe, never to return. An infinity of solitude but with God.

Kerry, "This Is my destiny. It Is clear that I have known from an early age that I was different.

Hello Reader,

    Come a long way in a short time. The fact is, could this be the reality of mental illness? Today we are all too quick to say *yes* but this is an individual's journey and who is to say this is not possible? There is a fine line in all our individuals' dimensions. We are all unique. Kerry's reality involves momentous changes with our planet Earth, and at this point the elite are not revealing the truth.

    Back, to the Truth...

Act 5

The skies are changing. The spectrum of light is shifting, as humanoids, we preserve darkness in the spectrum when the sun is not up but in this spectrum there is light. This Is becoming more visible to the population.

We're slipping into a mini ice age globally. there will be no escape from this by anyone. Fluctuations in the Exosphere and Ionosphere are detected by satellites and radio astrophysical observatory's.

"We're in trouble, Kerry, Louise clasps both Kerry's hands "Come with me now!"

Out of the back door of 212 they run.

Louise is panting, "They're going to section you. We cannot let this happen. They're trying to cover their mistakes, not that it matters now. It's too late for allot of people across the Earth."

"I'm with you." whispers Terraustrall "Follow the guidance of Pedrllehart with Louise. We come together under the east moon."

As the night falls, a crisp, cold Kerry and Louise have found an old squat for shelter, overnight.

Louise: "We need to make our way to London. There are believers there too but Kerry, we have to stay calm and blend in. we will catch the train tomorrow."

85 Albert Embankment, Lambeth, at a side door, rusted. On the steps to the basement, Louise knocks heavy on the door. It creeks open.

The man says, "Name please."

Louise stutters "Essavadore." The door opens to a brightly lit corridor.

"Come with me." The man beckons *this way*. "Wait here."

It's a small coffee room with brown leather settees and a single free coffee machine. Kerry starts shaking.

"It's OK" Louise calmly strokes his head "I'll get you a coffee. We're going to need It."

Twenty minutes pass and the door creeks open. There stands DR White.

"Hello there, you two. We need to talk. It was getting too risky in Cardiff, Kerry. Don't be afraid. Let me explain. It has come to our knowledge that Duirsail is in your bloodline. He is the only Skifakore to pass physically between dimensions he was your father, Kerry. Now you see why Louise bought you here? We need your DNA to synthesise the blood of our crew, piloting the craft Light Solar, so they can survive the dimensional travel jump. We need two of their light seeds of creation to correct our Earth. The testing of the dimensional engine by NASA for Light Solar started a irreversible deterioration in our orbit and this Is changing our climate. It might be a fact that this is an extinction level event. There is a medical centre here. We will get started in a couple of hours. Don't be afraid Kerry, we will take good care of you as you are the saviour from Duirsail."

Duirsail: "You're my devil. Step by step killing me. Overlord, dark days, your mind shredded, neurones clasp. Be away from me heathen! Shredded skin, the millennium seeing all before Christ. My flesh no more. Demons! they come forth the age in the age of death! Shout your mind, this begins. The stallions of justice shed your blood to the ground this history. Coming star to the valley under the bridge. The truth darker day today you see. Dream-state, visualisation Armageddon. We smile your happiness clean. D.N.A shredded. Bonded to the trees. Laugh now, no religion. Winged humanoids of peace bring the seeds to the stone touching wounds to heal. You see, we can love? You see we can be one in this struggle to paradise."

The glass door opens and in walks a giant of a man built like a brick wall with tight blonde curly hair. He speaks.

"OK Louise go. You can report for debrief. Off you go."

"Bye Kerry," as Louise hugs him.

Kerry confused looks at this man.

"I have heard your voice." He says

"Yes I'm on your team to look after you. My name's Stag, Peter Lewis to you. We only need a pint of your blood to start. The fact is, we need to get you state side as quick as possible. We have a jet on standby. We will be leaving in two hours. Get some descent food. You are a part of our last hope. Skifakore are guiding us all. Pray to God we get this right. We're going to knock you out for a few days. It's to get you rested as much as possible. Just a small injection and by the time you wake up we will be at NASA. You will just have to trust us. You have no other alternative. Come this way now."

Kerry Is led to a cell with brick walls. One window with bars and a concrete plinth in the middle of the room

"Lay down there on your stomach." says Peter and take your jeans off, a nurse walks in and gives Kerry an injection. Dazed and confused Kerry falls unconscious. What seems like seconds later Kerry hears,

"Wake up! Wake up! You're OK so don't worry."

It takes a few seconds as Kerry is coming around

"Where am I?" He says.

An American voice says "You're state side. Area 4, level three NASA headquarters."

He opens his eyes. Bright lights everywhere. "I thought I was dead." He says.

Peter says "Get a shower and some breakfast. We need to introduce you to your crew."

"My crew?" Kerry asks.

"Yes your crew! Your the only soul we can confirm who will survive the dimensional jump. Your blood is being synthesised and transfused t, your crew. Now get yourself together we need to step this up you have thirty minutes. Lets go Kerry." As he is led down a small corridor. "This is hanger No. 2 and here we have Light Solar, our dimensional travel vehicle. Kerry looks upon this majestic craft, dark purple no windows and smooth as air.

Act 6

"Here's your crew, Kerry. may I introduce you to Eris Leslie Jowett, Mathematician, Occupational Therapist Dione Jennifer Ennos, Nurse Practitioner, Computer Programmer. Rhea Dean Ekin, Mechanical Engineer, Forensic Sciences. Janus Edward Ryan, Human Resources Manager, Software Engineer."

At the moment Peter said Janus, Janus collapsed to the floor. The medics ran over. "He is dead." They stuttered. The transfusion must have reacted with his functions.

"Well that's a good start! You don't know how special you are, Kerry. You really need to come through on this." Kerry stood there shaking almost in tears.

"Pull yourself together." whispers Peter. "Let's get you suited up. The suits are organic hemp, man made fibres will melt."

They suit Kerry up, in what seems like a skin tight swimsuit with ridges that covers the complete body except for a small opening in the top of the head piece.

"We have no choice we need to get going as the crew are led to embark the craft."

Light Solar. Kerry touches the fuselage. Soft as skin and the deepest purple. Not a joint in site. He climbs the steps and sees that the cockpit is dimly lit by led lights. Five seats in a circular configuration, with a single control panel at the centre. As they were settled in by the ground crew, they were attached to oxygen. The control panel was not very large and looked like a music mixing desk but touch screen.

The door Is sealed by the crew and Kerry starts to panic in a cold sweat.

"I don't think I can do this." He says.

Eris replies "We're all here, Kerry. We just need faith. The universe is working through us. Relax. Take some deep breaths."

The craft is lifted on jacks and convoyed out to the launch site in only minutes but it felt like hours to the crew.

"We only need the engines at 45% to make the jump. It's all automatic. Any stronger and it will upset Earths polarity even more.

Eris: "Alexia, engage auto sequence."

Alexia: "Auto sequence activated."

Thirty seconds counted down but it seemed like hours. The hum of the engines kicked In.

Kerry was sweating but said "Lets do this!" Silence fell upon them all. No noise, just blurred vision, waves of multi coloured mists pulsed through the cockpit. A peace came over the crew but visions of being ripped apart by shock waves, the noise of the engines came back.

Eris "Alexia, status Jump complete."

Kerry was shocked and all he said "we have not moved."

Rhea: "Eris crack the hatch. We need to see this."

The hatch eased open and bright sun light cleared the darkness.

"Get me out of this seat!" shouted Kerry. "I don't feel too good"

slowly they all climbed down the steps, out of Light Solar. Kerry hit the floor on his knees.

"The pain! The pain in my back! What's happening?

Roots of bone started breaking out of his suite.

"We could not tell you Kerry. You are one of the Skifakore. You guided Louise whilst you were sleeping. They're your wings growing back. This is your dimension. Your real name Is Pedrllehart. Kerry, stay calm don't fight what's happening."

The landscape. Essavadore. Forests upon forests. Shadows started appearing above.

"They're here."

Circling down Terraustrall lands and places her hands upon Kerry's head. "It won't hurt for long child."

Within minutes Kerry has his wings. Brown feathers. Strong and proud wings. Terraustrall gathers him in her arms.

"You are my son." she says "You're back home. You are Earths only hope, Pedrllehart. We need to send the seeds of life back to their dimension. To mount Sirius, to stabilize their life energy. Berithdawe is coming with the seeds now. You soul has been away from you, Kerry gathering the knowledge of creation, the human dimension of Earth cannot sustain itself for much longer the last passing in the age of the last Pharaoh Cleopatra VII and the destruction of the Lighthouse of Alexandria. It contained the seeds of life. We fell back to Mount Sirius, created the inner temple of peace, the seeds depreciate as you can gather from human history. The darkness envelopes our creators will of peace. We must correct the instability and now this dimensional craft that the humans have created can offer the solution but it's destructive power can only be used once a millennia. We lost our power to carry the seeds through our dimensional portals. The universal galaxy that we draw our powers from is weakening. As it expands, all life must come to an end, to be created once more. Our time is coming to an end but this cannot be measured. It's our hearts telling us something of the spiritual has died. God created so we could learn and gather knowledge. When a society peaks in technology, the spiritual resets to create different pathways to seek knowledge that has not been addressed. The heart feeds off the mind and the mind feeds off the heart. We are carriers of the truth, hidden in the craft of the Skifakore will continue for our guides we need to pass our processes and knowledge to all dimensions We know this is never ending, but progressive. And as we die life and our practise will continue humans will never be able to obtain this status. We know of three dimensions that will achieve. Humans need to come back to themselves as dependent children of God. The human basic principle cannot gather past their own thoughts. They have mental and physiological blocks so the understanding will never be there. Earth was once heaven for all dimensions. The masses need to be informed that Earth has an elite who manipulate everything for their own gain. We do not need dictators from secret sociality breeds. The seeds will guide you, Pedrllehart. Through the magnetic fields there is only one spoken word to open the temple just say *forgiveness* and it shall pass to open the core of the mountain place. The seeds are on the offering pillars at each end of the temple."

Berithdawe comes circling to land "Leaves encase the seeds. Do not unwrap until the placement in the temple, Pedrllehart. Carry with care back to the dimensional craft. Now, peace be with . Do not fail.

Pedrllehart and the crew take there seats and put their oxygen on.

"close the hatch, Alexia and jump sequence."

"Jump sequence activated. Countdown commenced.

With light emitting from the seeds the engines start humming. The rainbow mist flows into the cockpit then drops off and the engines shut down.

"Alexia, Jump sequence complete. Open the hatch" says Eris.

The hatch opens and a bleak landscape, frozen and covered in ice greets then.

Pedrllehart struggles to get out of the hatch with the seeds. His wings intact, slowly beating. The NASA ground crew come out of the hanger.

"You have been gone for months. We were losing hope. Earth has gone into an ice age. We have been on lock down."

"I have no time." Pedrllehart spreads his wings, "I can do this. I know this vision changes. I can see electricity waves of guiding lines." He beats his wings faster and faster, suddenly takes off. Not aware of any other surroundings.

"Follow you heart." he can hear Terraustrall calling for him.

"Follow your heart. Age comes today, flight of Pedrllehart makes history."

Three days flying the skies, he comes upon the mount and lands. "Forgiveness" He says softly and the mountain opens. The temple is revealed. 12 stones on plinths, two empty.

"Place the seeds," He hears.

Either end of the temple, watery balls just like bubbles but black,

"Remove then replace them." He takes the seeds out of the leaves and replaces either end of the temple. A vibration surrounds him and electricity fills the room. The seeds glowing gold with the vision of Pedrllehart. He sees a mass gathering of electrical fusion. A calmness covers the room.

"Pedrllehart. Leave now." He hears.

Pedrllehart sores upwards, blinded by electricity waves and the mount closes upon itself. Instantly the ice begins to melt.

Act 7

As Pedrllehart flies not knowing where he is going, just following electrical pathways. The skies turn crimson, deeper than any colour in waves of the clouds. The winds are strong. The atmosphere is changing, beginning to breathe easier. Time comes back to the Earth.

Fluctuating waves of heat slowly warming the very souls of the human race. "I need food and water" thinks Pedrllehart, coming closer to the reality that he might not survive this planet. He sees land on the horizon, Madagascar, but there is still ice there has he lands on the shore.

Antanosy people came out of their dwellings, as some watched him land. "I need food water and shelter please help."

They did not understand so he tried hand gestures they took him down a path to what looked like a bomb shelter. Two days huddled in a corner as the locals sat and watched.

There came a thundering of Merlin helicopters landing on the beach. Moments later Royal Marines came through the opening.

"Kerry! Kerry! Come with us now were off HMS Bulwark you had a tracking devise In your suite."

Two of the marines picked him up and carried him out to the helicopters. Jimi Hendrix, Little Wing Is playing on the helicopters speakers, Safely in the ship's medical bay, the ships Doctor gave the all clear and administrated fluids.

Twenty four days sailing, the helicopters came within reach of London. Kerry Is airlifted to 85 Albert Embankment, Lambeth, Peter Lewis greats him.

"Good to see you, Kerry. Lou wants to see you. I'm sorry we will have to remove your wings this was a covert operation. Earth has been n a deep cold winter and from your success were coming around to liveable conditions again. The elitists have been well looked after n there bunkers. We have decided to seal their doors and let them live out there lives there. We even thought about shutting their oxygen supply off as they deserted everyone in need. A great struggle to stay alive Kerry."

As he is placed on a medical trolley and an injection knocks him out, a surgeon amputates his wings. Kerry falls into a coma, Louise stays by his bed playing music to him and reading story's.

This time turns out to be the start of world war, as country's including Russia and America want Kerry for themselves there was no hiding him. As London is bombed from all sides there is always money and excuses for war. It's the machine of death. We come away looking down on Kerry the facility has no roof as we pan away from this reality the world is lost again.

The Beginning.

© Nicholas Leslie MMXVII

Fly Skifakore

Shallow the dream ray of light, crossing paths together to become one more step closeness together.

Throw the hate to the pit forgetfulness help the dreams do not fail to the one the one only you

Blaze embers burn screaming the sky falling to the earth for you darkness sheered ripped by the thought.

Melted together essence of flesh warm glowing skin unwrapped emotions become to the one we are leaves falling from the gentle warm breeze.

Seasons turn to thoughts of love old with time impact interruptions of the mind, where are we be upon the wind fly Skifakore.

© Nicholas Leslie MMXVII

#ProgressivePoetry

Terraustrall

Come on the pathway light, the way we see we need less of the lonely world guardian come from cloudscapes of your mind. Hold me tight in this west wind hold your feelings In comfort escape Earth movements In time, cease oppression embrace truth speak truth fallen to the feet demonic ages comes down.

We who travel sleep the highways of light open your thoughts to love peace will never have the way of man sacrificed to history. On order no more maiestas folding cosmos we had a thought can we feel loved as one attest.

No hell or heaven humanity distortion we are children In our mothers eyes, listen to your hearts forgotten ones seventh appearers save your soul, Terraustrall broken wings I love you speaking softly see me open arms.

Embrace knowledge walking dimensions human kindness bring forth today Mammalium takes this world sheer fallen wings soil bound this millennia, twenty five thousand years the masters judgement on mankind God save you.

© Nicholas Leslie MMXVII

#ProgressivePoetry

Fragile

Show the care, infinite sequence In destruction hate darkness. We can be light, we can dance the tundra of your minds. Rainbows flow the crescent our hearts.

Many times sanctioned where they go, I give you strength. Holding you through the night sunrise comes no more fear. Grasp this time, never holding fast It's life's crime.

Loving you wrapped In my wings be soft my woman, this flesh Is not long touch my soul In this escape, the moment that's lost for many, us both.

Storm force escaped tilde worlds, In chaos bringing to begin. Years pass to forgetfulness never In regret hold fast don't cry. Search my mind I find you there as seasons change.

Winter Is the war to many souls your choice were free. On the way to heaven our universe ways In calm storms. Comfort, were so fragile bring me your name.

© **Nicholas Leslie MMXVII**

#ProgressivePoetry

Keys

Stretched across to your heart where Is the light a flower In life daydreams of peace bring us peace new beginnings my friend, soul projection for your morning sunrise tones.

In assent we are equal change the world true forms our minds rich of forgiveness take your swords to injustice following honesty to many fallen once care direction of this universe.

Goodbye to freedom intervention keys of light stranded In stone never fear bare emotions, entangled interned powers of magnitude carry yourself light be everything follow form.

Seconds In a dream hold tight echoes my fallout of devastation In mass you are the world we throned for justice the land falls to oceans conquering hearts nevermore time Is called.

© Nicholas Leslie MMXVII

#ProgressivePoetry

Be Free

With nothing I came to you in the shadow of war endless war pierced through the mind scream for your freedom chains hold golden sun rays scorch your eyes you will never see incendiary, Gods given you today they give to receive for death upon humanity. The children die untouched from skies of rain water flowing blood we all pass this day never-ending circles of hate greed, inhuman barren men Death watches over me whispering your names we pray no suffering.

Our fathers bones come to dust killers the barbarians telling lies, there was no love we see nations crumble ripping light from our heart from the sky passing by In your mistake never seeing comfort comes rise the new day our universe comes home to nurture our spirits you feel no singularity, can make you see closed minds In pain tortured thinking you have no feelings ripped inside out give your love.

Slowly walk with me In no direction In God's way never-ending point truth enter doors of light take the swords of salvation cast evil to death no return crimson butterfly's carry our hope delicate vanishing In lightning light. Your hope fades to darkness no end dark matter holds us tight but then shadows hear Earth cry we can see shards angels In stones of peace let me heal you grasp thoughts make yourself see then act upon your soul.

© **Nicholas Leslie MMXVII**

#ProgressivePoetry

www.ingramcontent.com/pod-product-compliance
Lightning Source LLC
Chambersburg PA
CBHW050253230526
45470CB00005B/2246